For Cath N.S.
For Ashok Kachru Pandit, Musema She Hassan Yesuf and all ActionAid's children, remembering specially Gultno Aliye J.B.

The compiler's royalties in this book are being donated to ActionAid, Chard, Somerset, TA20 1BR

OXFORD
UNIVERSITY PRESS

Great Clarendon Street, Oxford OX2 6DP

Oxford University Press is a department of the University of Oxford. It furthers the University's objective of excellence in research, scholarship, and education by publishing worldwide in

Oxford New York

Auckland Cape Town Dar es Salaam Hong Kong Karachi Kuala Lumpur Madrid Melbourne Mexico City Nairobi New Delhi Shanghai Taipei Toronto

With offices in

Argentina Austria Brazil Chile Czech Republic France Greece Guatemala Hungary Italy Japan Poland Portugal Singapore South Korea Switzerland Thailand Turkey Ukraine Vietnam

Oxford is a registered trade mark of Oxford University Press in the UK and in certain other countries

First published 1992
This paperback edition 2006

British Library Cataloguing in Publication Data

Data available

ISBN-13: 978-0-19-276324-2
ISBN-10: 0-19-276324-5

10 9 8 7 6 5 4 3 2

Printed in China by Imago

Acknowledgements
Every effort has been made to trace and contact copyright holders before publication and we are grateful to all those who have granted us permission. We apologize for any inadvertent errors and will be pleased to rectify these at the earliest opportunity.

Arnold Adoff: 'My Mouth' from *Eats* (Lothrop Lee & Shepard Books, 1979) © Arnold Adoff 1979. Reprinted by permission of the author and Lothrop, Lee & Shepard Books, a division of William Morrow & Company, Inc. John Agard: 'Snow-cone' from *I Din Do Nuttin* (Bodley Head, 1979). Reprinted by kind permission of John Agard c/o Caroline Sheldon Literary Agency. Mary Ann Hoberman: 'Meg's Egg' from *Yellow Butter, Purple Jelly, Red Jam, Black Bread* (Viking, 1981) © 1981 by Mary Ann Hoberman, reprinted by permission of Gina Maccoby Literary Agency. Lucia & James Hymes, Jr: 'Oodles of Noodles' from *Oodles of Noodles* © 1964, by Addison-Wesley Longman Publishing Company, Inc. Reprinted with permission of the publisher. Leland B. Jacobs: 'Taste of Purple' from *Is Somewhere Always Far Away?* © 1967 by Leland B. Jacobs, © 1983 by Allan D. Jacobs. Reprinted by permission of Henry Holt and Company, Inc. John Kitching: 'I Like Cabbage', © 1991 John Kitching, first published in *Twinkle Twinkle Chocolate Bar* (OUP, 1991). Reprinted by permission of the author. Judith Nicholls: 'Brian's Picnic' and 'Popalong Hopcorn' © Judith Nicholls, first published in *Popcorn Pie* (Mary Glasgow Publications, 1988). Reprinted by permission of the author. Grace Nichols: 'Sugarcake Bubble' from *No Hickory, No Dickory, No Dock,* © John Agard and Grace Nichols 1991; 'Have a Mango' from *Come On Into My Tropical Garden* © Grace Nichols 1988. Reproduced with permission of Curtis Brown Group Ltd, London on behalf of Grace Nichols. Jack Prelutsky: 'Chocolate Milk' from *Rainy Day Saturday* (Greenwillow Books, a division of William Morrow & Company) © Jack Prelutsky 1980. Clive Riche: 'The Wobbling Race', © 1991 Clive Riche, first published in *Twinkle Twinkle Chocolate Bar* (OUP, 1991). Reprinted by permission of the author.

OXFORD
UNIVERSITY PRESS

Meg's egg

Meg
Likes
A *reg*ular egg
Not a poached
Or a fried
But a *reg*ular egg
Not a devilled
Or coddled
Or scrambled
Or boiled
But an *egg*ular egg
*Meg*ular
*Reg*ular
Egg!

Mary Ann Hoberman

MEG

Sugarcake bubble

Sugarcake, Sugarcake
    Bubbling in a pot
Bubble, Bubble Sugarcake
    Bubble thick and hot

Sugarcake, Sugarcake
    Spice and coconut
Sweet and sticky
    Brown and gooey

I could eat the lot.

Grace Nichols

350g sugar
175 ml wate
Granada
St Kitts
nuts

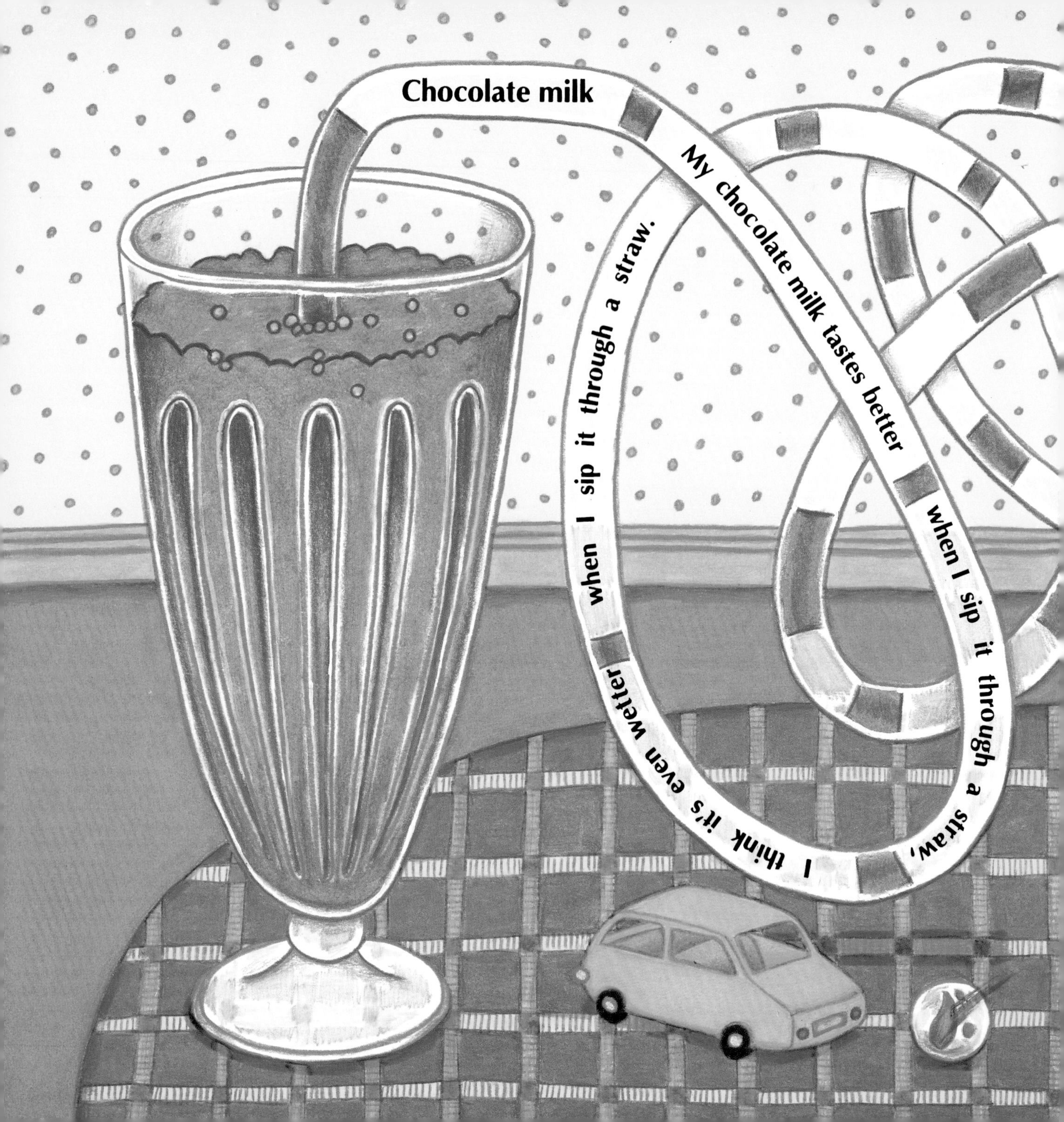
Chocolate milk
My chocolate milk tastes better
when I sip it through a straw,
I think it's even wetter
when I sip it through a straw.

Jack Prelutsky
With one end in the chocolate milk,
the other at my lips,
I drink up every single drop
with little tickling sips.

Taste of purple

Grapes hang purple
In their bunches,
Ready for
September lunches.
Gather them, no
minutes wasting.
Purple is
Delicious tasting.

Leland B. Jacobs

Oodles of noodles

I love noodles. Give me oodles.
Make a mound up to the sun.
Noodles are my favourite foodles.
I eat noodles by the ton.

Lucia & James L. Hymes, Jr.

Chocolate
CUSTARD POWDER
MUSTARD

I like cabbage

I like eating cabbage,
Turnip, beetroot, cress,
Very smelly foreign cheese,
And, best, (you'll never guess)
It isn't chocolate or ice-cream,
No, no, it isn't custard,
My very best, my favourite food,
Is sausages with mustard.

John Kitching

Snow-cone

Snow-cone nice
Snow-cone sweet
Snow-cone is crush ice
and good for the heat.

When sun really hot
and I thirsty a lot,
Me alone,
Yes me alone,
could eat ten snow-cone.

If you think is lie I tell
wait till you hear the snow-cone bell,
wait till you hear the snow-cone bell.

John Agard

Brian's picnic

We've . . .
cheese rolls, chicken rolls,
beef rolls, ham;
choose now, quickly, Brian —
bacon, beans or Spam?

I WANT A DOUGHNUT!

We've . . .
egg and cress and sausages,
good old lettuce leaf;
come on, Brian, take some now —
there's turkey, tuna, beef . . .

I WANT A DOUGHNUT!

We've . . .
treacle tart and apple tart,
biscuits, blackberries, cake —
Take which one you feel like,
Brian, come along now, take!

I WANT A DOUGHNUT!

There's . . .
jelly next or trifle,
everything must go!
Quickly, Brian, pass your plate —
is it yes or no?

I WANT A DOUGHNUT!

LAST CHANCE!

We've . . .
sponge cake, fruit cake,
eat it *any* way!
Peanut butter, best rump steak . . .
what is that you say?

I WANT A DOUGHNUT!

Judith Nicholls

nice
nice

The wobbling race

Two jellies had a wobbling race
To see who was the wibbliest.
Then the sun came out and melted them
And made them both the dribbliest.

Clive Riche

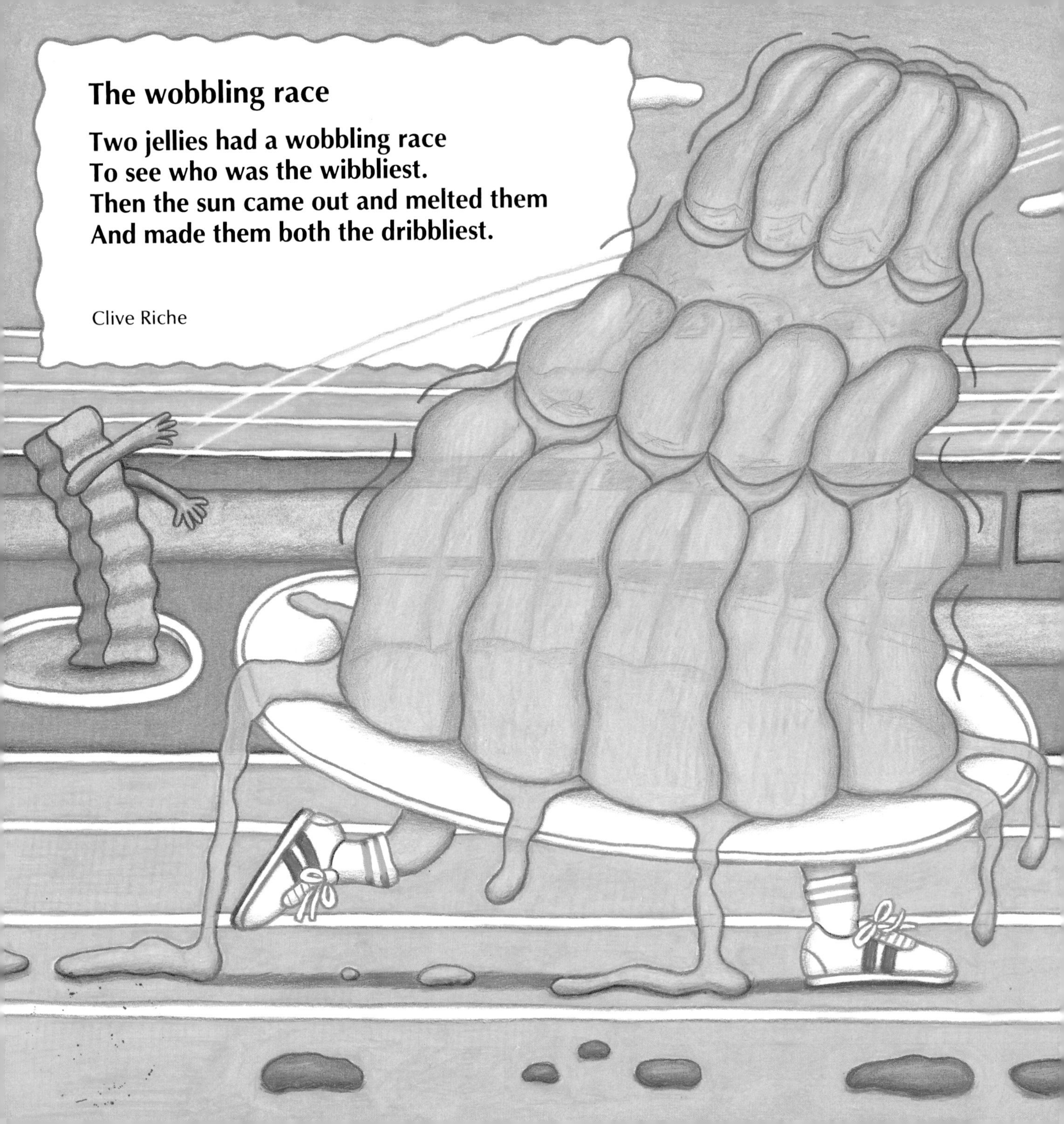

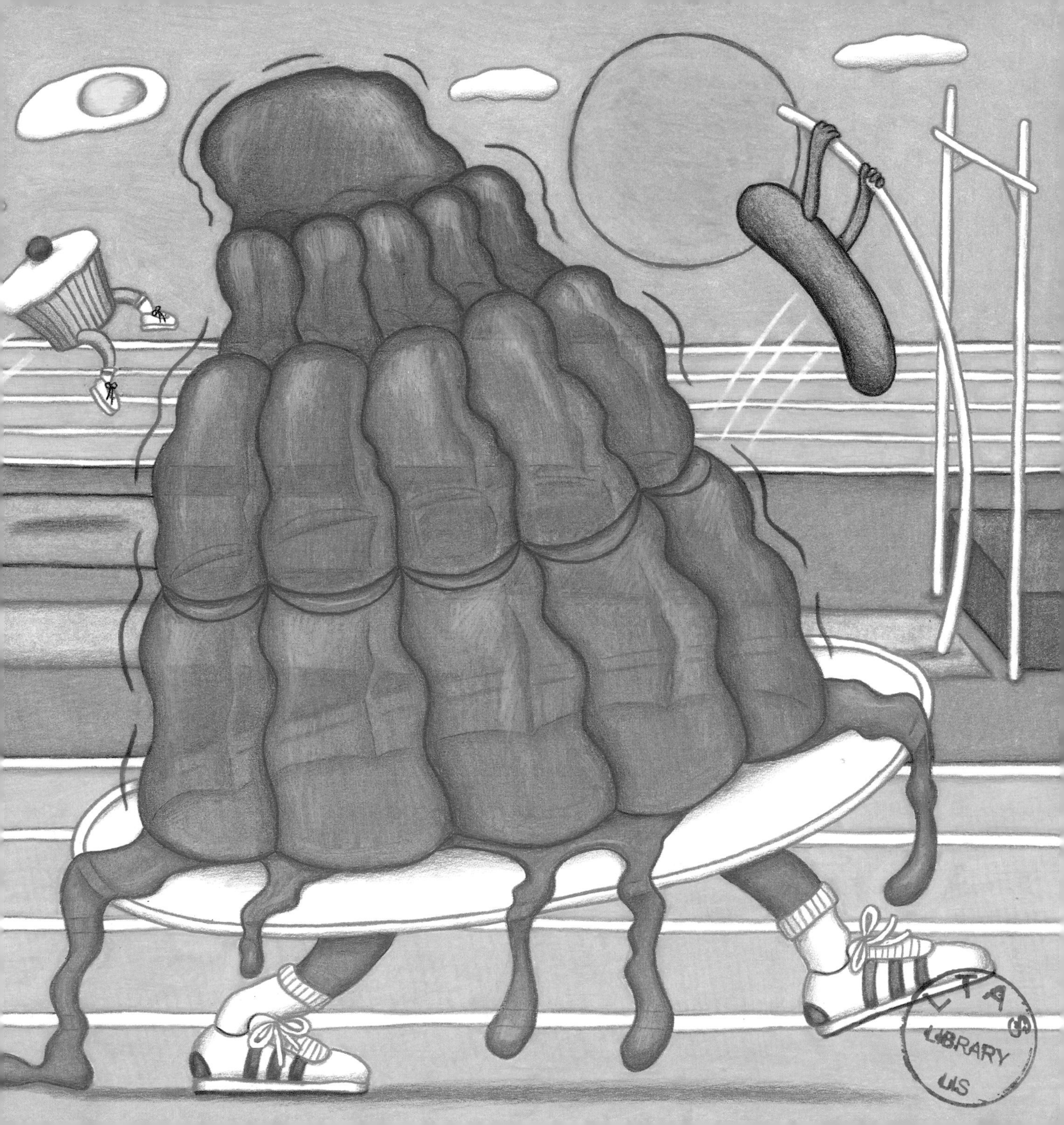

Have a mango

Have a mango
sweet rainwashed
sunripe mango
that the birds
themselves
woulda pick
if only they
had seen it —
a rosy miracle

Here

take it from mih hand.

Grace Nichols

Popalong hopcorn!

I'm a hopalong
popalong
popcorn in the pan!
In
out
up
down!
Catch me
if
you
can!

Judith Nicholls

POP
CORN

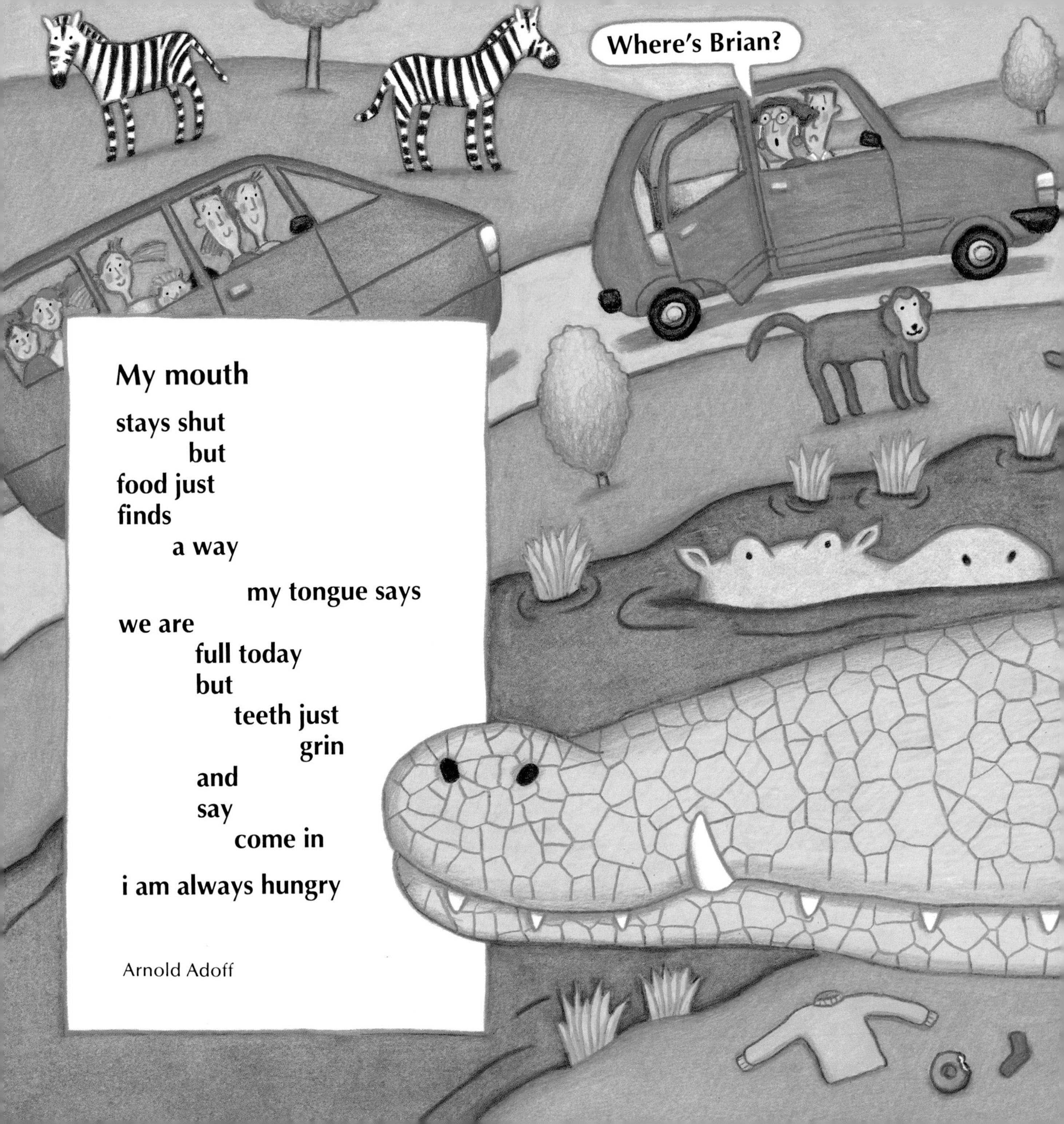

My mouth

stays shut
        but
food just
finds
    a way

            my tongue says
we are
        full today
        but
            teeth just
                grin
        and
        say
            come in

i am always hungry

Arnold Adoff

STAY IN
YOUR CAR!